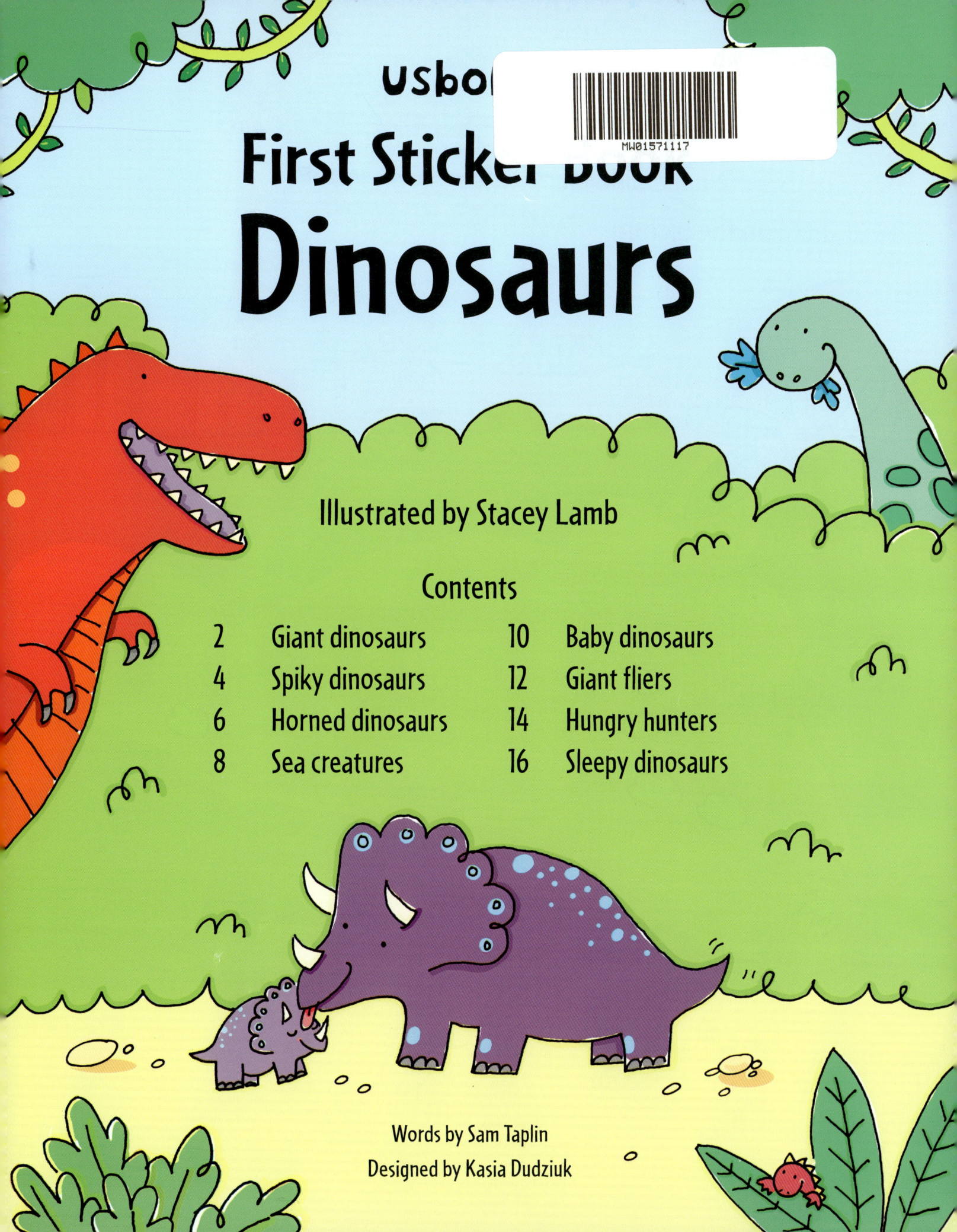

Giant dinosaurs

Sauropods were huge dinosaurs with very long necks. Stick them on the picture.

Horned dinosaurs

Triceratops had three horns on its head. Add lots of them to this picture.

Sea creatures

When the dinosaurs lived on the land, amazing animals lived under the sea. Fill the water with sea creatures.

Horned dinosaurs

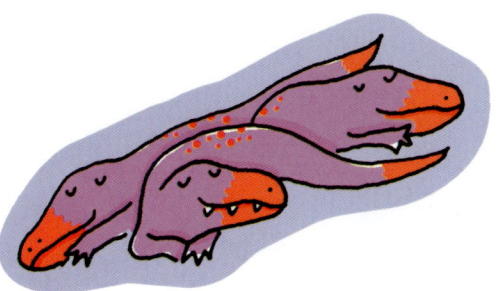

Sea creatures

Baby dinosaurs

Sleepy dinosaurs

Baby dinosaurs

Some dinosaurs made nests and laid their eggs in them. Stick eggs and babies in the nests.

Giant fliers

Big creatures with wings lived at the same time as the dinosaurs. Fill the sky with them.

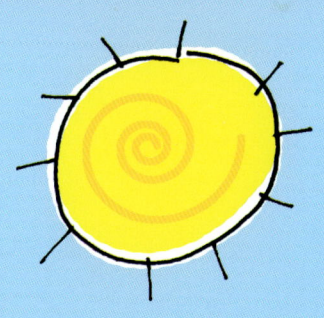

Hungry hunters

Tyrannosaurus rex was a fierce dinosaur that ate other dinosaurs. Add three to this picture.

Sleepy dinosaurs
Fill this page with lots of sleepy dinosaurs.